Mighty Writing
College Application
Essay Guide

Everyone has a story to tell.

Make yours mighty.

By Laurie Filipelli

in collaboration with Irena Smith

Sources for quotes and additional reading
MightyWriting.org/resources

Published by MightyWriting, LLC in Austin, Texas.
More College App Essay Tips and Tools at MightyWriting.org

Revised and edited in collaboration with Irena Smith, Ph.D. from
IrenaSmithConsulting.com.

Cover design, book design, photographs and formatting
by Mario Champion from brighterplanet.org.

Special thanks to my mentor, Irena Smith, to Emma Olson and
Mara Smith who acted as student readers, to Mario Champion for
his design work, and to all the students who've entrusted me to
help them along on their writing journeys.

Testimonials

"This is an expert, engaging, and truly helpful guide for any student staring down the "mouth of hell" —the daunting college application essay process."

    —Katherine Ellison, Pulitzer Prize-winning journalist and author of "Buzz: A Year of Paying Attention."

"Writing is an art. It is a skill honed with exposure to the best writing, and, more importantly, with guidance on how to tailor your unique expression. Irena and Laurie are wizards with words: they helped me crystallize verbose sentences and infuse them with new meaning and impact. I love most that their guidance is empowering. It enables and equips you to chart out a beautiful piece of writing that tells your story. This confidence and self-reflection is necessary going into an essay-writing process. Above all, their warmth, dedication, and collaborative approach made my application process a very memorable experience, one that I shall cherish forever."

    —Student, Duke University

"Irena and Laurie guided me through the process of expressing my own voice and helped me express that voice most clearly and impactfully. Their advice was always clear—not only did they advise what I needed to work on, they also helped me with *how* to go about it, which is usually where I get stuck. Working with Laurie and Irena was more than writing a college essay—they also really pushed me to really reflect and be honest with myself, which ultimately helped me gain a deeper understanding of who I was and what I wanted to do."

> —Student, Harvard University

"I truly believe that Laurie's insightful questions made my son's essays come alive. I don't think he would have achieved the same results without her. Not only was he accepted at his first choice school, but he was given the Rensselaer Leadership Award which is a four-year merit scholarship."

> — Parent, Rensselaer Polytechnic Institute student

"This book was super helpful! I read through it in one sitting and now have a million things I could write about. Laurie and Irena's compelling and easy-to-follow advice gave me confidence and inspired me to try the exercises not because I had to, but because it was fun. "

> —Student, Austin Waldorf High School

TABLE OF CONTENTS

FOREWORD by Irena Smith

If you're contemplating the college application process, you may well feel like you're staring down into the mouth of hell. Standardized tests, teacher letters of recommendation, AP courses, activity lists, college visits, alumni interviews, fine arts supplements, the personal statement, supplementary essays—it goes on and on. Luckily, there are excellent resources out there to help you make sense of all the moving parts. This book isn't one of them; rather, it's an in-depth guide to demystifying and mastering the writing part of the application: the long and short essays that ask you to respond to a dizzying barrage of prompts, but that are really inviting you to answer multiple variations of the same question: "Tell us more about yourself." Approached in the right spirit, with a sense of openness and adventure, writing these essays—and discovering who you are really, apart from your grades and scores and activity list—can be a rite of passage. It's an opportunity to dig deep and look inward and at the same time to look forward, to the self you dream of becoming.

This guide was born of six years (and counting) of collaboration during which Laurie and I worked together with dozens of students on brainstorming, crafting, and revising college essays. Together, we oversee the essays from inception to completion, a process informed by our experience teaching, writing, and working in admissions. As we help each of our students uncover deeper layers of significance in the stories that unfold in each successive draft, we engage in a vibrant and spirited exchange that is both inspiring and invigorating. We want to continue that conversation here, because as longtime educators (between the two of us, we have over three decades of experience teaching literature and composition at the high school and college level), passionate readers, and committed writers we believe that the essay is much more than yet another cog in the larger machine of your application.

Your journey toward completing the college essay may not be a literal journey (after all, there's not much physical movement in putting pen to paper or, more likely, fingers to keyboard), but it can be mapped. If you've ever watched *Buffy the Vampire Slayer* or read *Harry Potter* or *The Hobbit*, the arc goes something like this: the hero descends into a grim and perilous underworld, one which puts his (or her) ingenuity, courage, and resolve to the test, and emerges triumphant after conquering daunting obstacles and dangerous adversaries. My favorite such plot line occurs toward the end of Philip Pullman's *The Amber Spyglass,* in which Lyra, the teenage heroine, calls upon her courage and wit to navigate the underworld where she manages to entrance both the legions of the dead and the fearsome harpies who torment them by telling stories about her childhood adventures. The harpies, spellbound, refrain from tearing at Lyra's face and eyes, and when she asks why, the chief harpy responds: "Because [the story] was nourishing. Because it was feeding us. Because we couldn't help it. Because it was true. Because we had no idea that there was anything but wickedness. Because it brought us news of the world and the sun and the wind and the rain. Because it was true."

Replace Lyra with a high school student, the underworld with the angst-filled first semester of senior year, the harpies with nameless, faceless, terrifying admissions officers, "eager and hungry and suffused with the lust for misery," and you have a pretty accurate picture of the college application process. Except not really. I was a college admissions officer for four years, and I don't think of myself as particularly terrifying. I'm 5'1" (on a good day), I default to yoga pants when I can get away with it, and I am known for my skewed yogurt to topping ratio at frozen yogurt shops. In other words, I'm a real human person, not a harpy. And while you may not think of yourself as a hero, I can promise that you too will emerge into the bright, triumphant promise of second semester senior year, wiser, stronger, and changed for the better by the opportunity to reflect on who you are and put words to your story.

But you're not there yet, and like Lyra at the threshold of the underworld, you're probably terrified by what lies ahead. You probably have a ton of questions. How do you talk about yourself without bragging? What if your story is trivial, or unexciting, or TMI? What if your friend is funny and you're serious and you're worried that her essay is going to be fun to read and yours is going to put your reader to sleep? Should you write about the time you tore your ACL and couldn't play basketball, or about your trip to Costa Rica, or your grandmother, or your divorced parents? If you've gone to a college information session, you may have been told not to write on certain subjects (sports, grandparents, service trips, divorce), and you might be feeling paralyzed, because one of those four (or all of them, if you're going through a particularly tumultuous time) feels like your whole life right now, and if you can't write about those things, what can you write about?

This is a book whose purpose is to help you find, and tell, your best stories—stories that are true, no matter what anyone says. Stories that reflect your own experience of the world. Stories that will let the reader into your reality and forge a connection, even if you may never meet the person who reads your application.

Admissions officers do share one thing in common with the harpies: they love stories, and evaluating applications feels like sitting down to a never-ending feast. Every day brings a different flavor of story: wrenching, funny, sweet, sharp. There are stories about watching cooking shows for six months straight while quarantined for a serious illness. Stories about an inadvertent haircut with larger-than-expected consequences. Stories about a summer job that turned out to be an unexpected lesson in social and economic inequality. Stories about parents, grandparents, siblings, rowing, football, fencing, soccer, singing, running, improv, dumplings, pie, a dried plant collection, a grade-school sculpture gone terribly wrong, board games, American Sign Language, Indian classical dancing, interior decorating, math tutoring, philosophy.... and I could go on.

Not only do admissions officers really, really like stories, they really, really like teenagers. They like their fizzy energy, their boundless optimism, the infinite possibilities before them. And they love getting to know them through their essays. They're on your side. They want to hear what you have to say.

The journey you're about to embark on is a difficult one, no doubt about it. Benjamin Franklin said it best: "There are three things extremely hard: steel, a diamond, and to know one's self." But we very much hope that as you complete your journey, you will experience not just the difficulty, but also the joy—the exhilaration, really—of word by word, sentence by sentence, paragraph by paragraph, finding, and articulating, your own truths.

Tell us about your world.

PREFACE by Laurie Filipelli

College application essays offer the chance to present who you are, in all of your particular splendor. To own that splendor is no easy task: sometimes the gems right in front of you are buried deep beneath a pile of expectations and commitments and doubt.

The truth, however, is simple: you just need to dig them up. In other words, you have a life, and that life is full of stories.

Together, Irena and I work with students who are finding their way into college, not solely through improving test scores or bolstering their list of activities, but by expressing their truest selves: students who write for school papers, who struggle with dyslexia, who battle scorpions in Texas, search for mushrooms in Oregon, or jog Central Park religiously each day. We get to know them all, and in knowing them, like them immensely. We cheer them on, offering tips from the sidelines—we love being part of a team.

This guide itself is an example of teamwork. I drafted the following exercises as a series of blog posts, and together we clarified a vision, coauthored new sections, scheduled weekly phone calls, and shared documents as we worked through revisions and edits.

We get it that writers need support, but it doesn't take five college counselors, an attentive AP English teacher, and a hands on in-person writing coach (though we love to coach in person!) to find which stories are most meaningful and to help you polish until their meaning shines. To compose compelling college admissions essays, it does help to have a map to guide you.

From pre-writing, that wonderful phase in which we bumble and make mistakes without pressure, to reading for inspiration, to several rounds of revision, to editing, this book will lead you on the journey of writing your life.

Before you take that first step, you might be wondering more about your destination—the elusive personal essay. To get the lay of the land, read on.

WHAT'S A PERSONAL ESSAY ANYHOW?

A personal essay is more than just an essay that about you. It's a form, just like a poem or a short story or a novel is a form, only it happens to be true. Or mostly true, or emotionally true, as writers like to say. In others words, it's OK to change the weather outside if you're recounting a horrible day, but it's not OK to totally make up the events that made it horrible. It's also more than OK to sound like you: that means many things you were taught not to do—use first person, make contractions, throw in slang, use fragments, start a sentence with "and" or "but"—are now the norm.

A good personal essay has little in common with the kind of five-paragraph argument you often write for English class and more in common with, well, a story. Like any good story, a personal essay will have a protagonist or a hero—and that hero is you! And, whether you trek to Mount Doom, Panem, or to the band practice room, there should be some kind of journey— a progression or discovery. Simply put, in the best personal essays, you begin in one place, and end in another.

But don't trust our assessment, read some personal narratives. Our favorite authors range from Annie Dillard to David Sedaris to Ta-Nehisi Coates. You can also find inspiration outside of the literary realm. The autobiographies of political figures, rock stars, athletes, or the spontaneous stories that everyday people tell—without a script or even any notes for a series called The Moth at https://themoth.org/stories —teach us about urgency and authenticity. Check out our recommended reading list at http://MightyWriting.org/resources.

It may seem unconventional that NO student essays have made our list—we've certainly read some great ones—but we don't believe a quick approach in which you model your writing on another student's success works. Personal essays are not about marketing yourself (though it may feel that way when the stakes are high!), they are about knowing yourself. Our list is designed to inspire you toward your own truth.

But a word to the wise: be discerning about what you take away. A writer for *The New York Times* may focus on a marriage gone wrong, a memoirist may confess her alcoholism. But, these are not good topics for college application essays! We are sharing them because they are good and honest writing, full of engaging details and well-crafted sentences that can help light the way as you find your own best stories.

To be fair, we wouldn't want to lead you on a journey that we hadn't taken ourselves. So feel free to read our essays, too, at http://MightyWriting.org/resources.

Now, are you ready to get going?

CHAPTER 1– **INVITE YOURSELF TO GET STARTED**

Any writer worth their salt will tell that writing is equal parts freedom and self-imposed constraint. So, before you explore, get your GPS in place. Think of this as the How, When and Where of your essay writing invitation.

How:

You probably have a list of schools forming. Check out their essay requirements, and begin to organize the list into a form that includes prompts, word counts and deadlines as well. To make it easy, we've made this online College Essay Tracker at http://mightywriting.org/essaytracker for you.

The Tracker will prompt you to set up folders on your Google drive, which is a great way to allow for easy sharing, instant backup up, and online access to your work. However, we aren't here to promote Google—you could also make your own system. A folder for each school that lives on your desktop could work as well.

When:

Take a look at your deadlines and "back out" a writing schedule. Say your deadline is Nov. 1. Generally speaking, we recommend five drafts, and, if it takes a week per draft, that means starting in mid-September. But wait, if Nov. 1 is the deadline, you certainly want to submit at least a few days prior, right? And if September is the start of school, you may as well begin in August, right? Oh, and if you're attending a camp or working a summer job, better make that July, just to be safe! And, you're applying to *how many* schools??

The best answer may be simply be NOW, whenever now happens to be. *Note:* If now is October, don't imagine you've crushed your chances. You'll just need to prioritize—you can get this done!

Where:

Will you write in your room for 15 minutes each morning? At the dining room table for a few hours each Sunday? Do you have a favorite nook in the school library? One successful student wrote all his essays during off periods at school while his friends hung out. Rituals help, but don't be a slave to them. Writing on your phone in a burst of late-night inspiration is more than acceptable!

Time for Trust

"Trust thyself: every heart vibrates to that iron string." Ralph Waldo Emerson

Now that the outer shell is in place, set it aside. It's time for the inner work. As you move through the exercises in this book, you'll mine your experiences, examine possessions that hold meaning, and think through beliefs and dreams. Take your time. It may require several different exercises, along with a few long walks or heartfelt conversations, to uncover the true gems that will become your best essay topics. Once you feel a topic click, trust it. Your own story is worth telling! Don't let your internal editor tell you something is dumb or not not good enough. If it matters to you, it should matter to the reader.

No one is youer than you

As Dr. Seuss tells us, we are all worth celebrating. Because the subject of your essay is you, *you* are the expert. That's why this book includes no sample essays from enviable students admitted to Ivy League schools. That's right—none. Irena, an avid swimmer, likens avoiding reading other students' essays to the practice of sticking to your own lane. You can perfect your strokes by reading wonderful writing that falls into the genre of personal essay, but you need not ponder your direct competition—other successful students—and risk being thrown off your game. Just keep your eyes on the black line at the bottom of the pool. Tell your own story, like no one else can.

Invite others to the party

Sticking to your own lane, however, is not the same as going it alone. Writers, by nature, tend to be solitary people, but they also share ideas, provide honest feedback, and build on each other's hunches. In the end, while your essays are completely yours, your quest shouldn't occur alone. Ask teachers, parents, and friends to help you make sense of the stories you want to tell. Read to learn from other writers, and to find community with fictional characters whose journey either inspires you or reminds you of your own. Form a team with a best friend or that guy from English class.

Together you can brainstorm ideas and to keep each other on task.

If the going gets rough...
Finally, remember this book is here to help light the way, but you have other lights too. If it gets rocky, and you find yourself veering too far into darkness, ask for help. Sometimes writing brings up personally difficult material—it's natural—just move your essay out of your college application folder and keep writing. And return to this essay guide when you're ready.

Now, let's take the the next step together!

CHAPTER 2 – **THE POWER OF THE LIST**

Getting started on your college application essay is probably much easier than you think. You may have heard that you need to examine the prompts or even make a dreaded outline as a first step, but my guess is that advice didn't come from writers. What most writers will tell you is that they begin with inspiration, and that inspiration doesn't always come naturally. They trick themselves into finding it. One foolproof way is by making lists. Lists help you generate ideas, organize thoughts, and prioritize goals. Lists are low effort for big return. If getting started is the hardest parts of any task, then a list is the easiest way to go.

How? Try this.

10 DAYS / 10 LISTS

Use a notebook, a book that you've made, a writing app, or create a special folder on your desktop or drive. Set aside a regular time to write each day. It can be for as little as 10 minutes, first thing in the morning or right before you go to bed. Focus on events and images as much as thoughts and feelings.

It's time to get writing! For each list suggestion, set a timer for five minutes, and write as fast as you can. Don't get bogged down in whether an item is irrelevant or misspelled or slightly crazed. These aren't your application essays—these are building blocks that you'll sort through later in order to find durable, authentic, and, yes, even beautiful material.

1. Make a list of everyone you've ever known. (Seriously, see how many!)
2. Make a list of your favorite places (from continents to hidden nooks).
3. Make a list of what you carry in your backpack.
4. Make a list of your favorite time killers (blogs, Youtubers, books, apps, movies, and shows).
5. Make a list of your favorite foods.
6. Make a list based on something you consider yourself an expert on (cookie recipes, football stats, Star Wars characters, art supplies, whatever).
7. Make a list of things you learned just this year (from tying a slip knot, to using a semicolon, to learning to drive a car).

8. Make a list of things you'd love to do or learn. Again, anything goes: play the guitar, make your own clothes, hike the Appalachian trail, influence Congress, or get a sweet date for prom.

9. Make a list of people you'd like to thank (no need to know them personally, maybe better not to!) and what you'd like to thank them for.

10. Make a list of nice things people have said about you, and when and why they said it. (Don't be too modest. You are amazing!)

NEXT STEPS

Appreciate your lists:
You've now catalogued hundreds of people, places, ambitions, and experiences—the nuts and bolts that make up your life. Somewhere in there a few great stories are just waiting to emerge.

Find groupings (this part is mostly for fun, but also productive): Look back at each list, separately. Read the list aloud. Can you find groupings, e.g. when listing names did you list all of your aunts and uncles together? When listing foods did you separately out desserts, snacks, and meals? With people you'd like to thank, did you go in chronological order, or group family members separate from historical figures? Did your list of places include vacation spots, quiet corners, concert venues?

Dig deeper and tell a story (this part is a must): Again, one list at a time. Circle three items on your list that you could tell a story about. For example, if one of your favorite places is beneath a live oak tree in your neighborhood park, you might have a story about building fairy gardens there as a kid, or kicking back there with friends last weekend. If you included Malala Yousafzai or Mark Zuckerberg or mom in the list of people you'd like to thank, then answer the question, "why?"

Tip: For easy practice, have someone else randomly select a list item and then tell them a story about it.

10 FREEWRITES for 10 MINUTES EACH

Now ease into the writing process. Over a few days (or weeks if you've started early!) narrow your stories down and complete 10 freewrites about them. Remember, freewrites are meant to be unfettered. No revising now, no telling yourself it's stupid. Just keep your pen to the page (or your fingers to the keyboard) for 10 minutes, and write.

Tip: Keep in mind the mightiest stories often have the smallest subjects. You could write as intriguingly about your love of Legos as you could about visiting the Great Wall. You could write about the Metropolitan Museum of Art or a habit of doodling alongside your notes. What matters is that you notice and appreciate the world around you, and think about your role in it.

CHAPTER 3 – **START WITH AN IMAGE (not with a prompt!)**

If you did the exercises in Chapter 2, you may have noticed that your lists were full of images: important objects in your life from Kraft mac 'n cheese to the Stetson guitar a touring rock star left in your grandfather's taxi. Things we see, hear, touch, and smell make up our lives. As you begin drafting essays, images are a great place to start.

Images help you discover yourself—your stories, your beliefs, and your obsessions. Consider the following activities as different ways of gathering images as ingredients. Your essays will be meals you prepare later. So, seriously, put the prompts away for now. Let's first see what's in your image fridge. If you found plenty of inspiration with your Chapter 2 lists, you might skip this next part—or not—it's amazing how much material we all have hidden (and how many essays you may end up writing).

As you try out the exercises below, you might find that abstractions like "freedom" or "love" keep slipping onto your image shelf. For some clarification about the difference between abstraction and image, hit pause on this book and check out http://grammar.ccc.commnet.edu/grammar/composition/abstract.htm. Also check out the image guru, cartoonist Lynda Barry. She was my inspiration for the second activity.

CREATE A TIME CAPSULE

Grab an old shoebox—yep, a shoebox!—and fill it with cherished items that help define you.

Note: Of course, you could set up a folder in your Google drive/ Dropbox/ Pinterest/ Instagram and fill it with virtual stuff, but having objects to pull out and hold on to may make writing easier. Plus, you won't be distracted by everything online that has nothing at all to do with getting you into college!

Some possible things to include:
- Photos
- Song lyrics & book quotes
- Pictures cut from magazines or grabbed from favorite sites
- Souvenirs & lucky charms
- Tickets stubs
- Drawings, postcards, notes, letters

Then, set aside time, once or twice a week, to reach in and randomly grab something to write about. Set a timer for 10 minutes, grab a pen or a laptop and start by describing what you see. With any luck you'll then find yourself slipping into a story.

In my shoebox is a photo of me screaming my head off on a kids' roller coaster called "The Beastie." (It's actually kind of hilarious.) I start by describing the utter fear in my eyes, and the way the five-year-old girl behind me is waving her arms in pure joy. I then recount how my friend dragged me onto the ride, assuring me it would be fun. At some point, I reveal that I'm 28 in this photo. And who knows what reflections might happen from there? Something profound about fear—or taking chances? The idea is to ground yourself in imagery, and let it lead where it may.

Note: After your 10-minute freewrite, you might chose NOT to read over what you've written for a few days. Fresh eyes are always a help!

ANOTHER LIST!

Some of my favorite advice on how best to make lists comes from the cartoonist Lynda Barry. In a nutshell, she says, make a list of 5-10 images, things you came across during the day. Here's mine for today.

1. Moldy swim "noodle" at the YMCA
2. Endless traffic on S. Lamar Boulevard
3. A delicious looking ham and cheese crepe
4. Carefully piled coins on the dining room floor, next to an opened piggy bank (who knows what my daughter is saving up to buy?)
5. A girl and a giant robot near downtown

After that, choose one (or more) image to write about. The moldy swim noodle, for example, might become a journal entry about me in my first Aqua Yoga class, and how I had to get over the fact that the class is made up of almost entirely seniors (and I don't mean 12th graders). And, yep, I LOVED it. Endless traffic might turn into an entry about all the grand ideas my family and I have for solving Austin's traffic problems—our first being The Big Lift.

You get the idea? Before you know it, you'll have a sizable collection of strong and detailed stories.

START DRAFTING NOW! (Yes, actually now.)

Remember you're cooking, not just grabbing a snack. So gathering and prepping ingredients (images and stories) is essential. It will prepare you to serve up authentic essays that admissions folks find delicious. *Now* is a good time to check out your prompts. Chances are you'll be full of answers!

CHAPTER 4 – **MIRROR MIRROR**

Images can serve as a great entry point into college application essay writing. They reveal our distinct perceptions and often show us things about ourselves that may have been hidden: why our first iPod was so important, or the reason that the smell of coffee gives comfort, and so on.

Another way to know ourselves is to discover more about the outward image we present. This may sound terrifying at first, but it's not so bad if we turn to our closest friends and ask them to be our mirrors. You might be surprised and delighted by what you discover.

START TALKING

For this exercise, you'll start by talking with trusted friends and family members, jotting down notes as you go. Ask them the following questions, as well as a few questions of your own. No reply is too small or silly to be essay fodder!

- When they remember something funny or unusual or clever that you did, what do they remember? Sometimes these little defining stories can be the most important ones.

- When your friends or family members identify your character and your (perhaps hidden!) strengths, what do they say? Do they see you as funny or serious, quirky or sophisticated, silly or stoic, or...?

- What are they seeking when they come to you for help?

- What do you spontaneously contribute to the activity of a group?

Repeat this process with at least one other person, and don't forget to jot down notes!

START WRITING

Now, look over your notes, ask yourself questions, dig deeper, and write mightily! Some tips to help you along:

- Are there any trends emerging? Circle repeated phrases. Are there contradictions? Note those too. Then take 10 minutes to write freely in relation to any memories that connect with the attributes others see in you.

- Are there stories to be told? For example, your ability from age two to identify the make and model of any car on the road, your extraordinary patience with your younger sister, your skill at imitating voices and accents, your role as the "sheep herder" in the family, and a million more...

Remember, others often see us more clearly than we see ourselves. Their impressions can contribute to our own authentic reflection and lead us to our most memorable essays.

CHAPTER 5 – **SHOW US YOUR GENIUS!**

In Chapter 4 you uncovered your own own amazing character. Maybe you are funny, determined, poetic, methodical, or an incorrigible optimist. We each have our own kind of genius. But even though you're pretty terrific, you probably don't want to come straight out and brag in your college application essay.

That's where good writing comes in. Before you go on, read <u>this smart essay by Mark Moody</u> that Irena shared with me years ago. I often come back to his advice to "show" rather than "tell," and to not "waste precious time explaining."

A PICTURE IS WORTH...

As the old adage goes, a picture is worth a thousand words. Of course, as a writer you only have words to work with, but you can certainly learn to paint with them. Actually, you don't even have to be a self-proclaimed writer to do it. Here's the world famous boxer, Muhammad Ali, painting a quick portrait of his high school days:

> "As part of my boxing training, I would run down Fourth Street in downtown Louisville, darting in and out of local shops, taking just enough time to tell them I was training for the Olympics and I was going to win a gold medal. And when I came back home I was going to turn pro and become the world heavyweight champion in boxing. I never

thought of the possibility of failing—only of the fame and glory I was going to get when I won."

Note: The above is from an essay called "I Am Still the Greatest," from the NPR series This I Believe, a wonderful resource for personal essay writers.

Notice that without overtly stating how he felt—"I was confident" or "I was energetic" or "I was optimistic"—he reveals a world about his character. And this is key. It's tempting to create details about everything from your alarm clock going off in the morning to what you ate for dinner. But details shouldn't simply show for the sake of showing, they should reveal something important about you. And rest assured, you also have something important to show to admissions readers.

WE ALL HAVE OUR OWN GENIUS!

Now go ahead and pick an anecdote that reveals your brightest and best self. It can be a moment of accomplishment, a time you were afraid, or an experience of joy. Then, write it with details that help your reader to see it. With practice, this might be the introduction for a new essay.

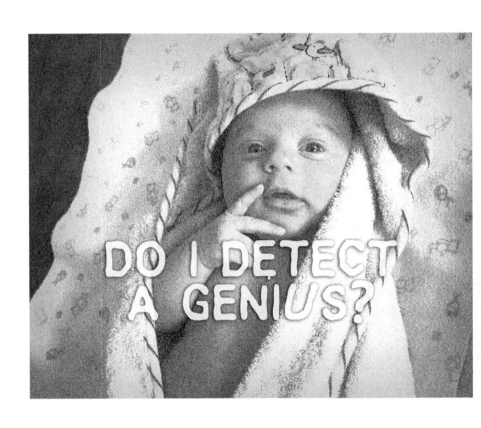

Interlude – Go Read a Book!

Even the mightiest writers needs a productive break from writing—the moment when you step away to examine what's in the fridge or stare out the window for the hundredth time. This may seem like procrastination, but I think of it as "moodling." (A term coined by a fiction writing friend to denote a combination of doodling and musing.) When you moodle, your brain rests and readies to receive the elusive idea you've been tracking. Many writers find their best ideas on long walks or when taking a shower. But perhaps the biggest inspiration is the one most often overlooked: reading.

Reading, any reading, can ready us to write by transitioning our brains into the realm of words. And, the best part? While you feel as if you're taking a break, your brain is actually working to become a better writer and a better thinker, too.

When I trained writers to teach in public schools we had a simple and foolproof equation that led students to become authors. Read. Write. Share. *First we'd read a literary snippet, then we'd write something of our own. Finally we'd share and elicit feedback. Writing isn't complicated. It's a craft, not a science, and like all crafts—from cooking to welding to tennis to calligraphy—it's not so much innate as it is learned through practice. Everything you read is writing practice.*

We've already suggested readings to help you get to know the genre of the personal essays at http://mightywriting.org/resources, but don't limit your reading to personal essays alone. Read omnivorously—fiction to get a sense of how story lines are constructed, poetry for emotional concision, non-fiction to get your arguments straight. And all of it to nurture your understanding of the world and inspire your own inner creator.

When you come back, your head may be full of new images, your sentences new rhythms, and your ideas will inevitably flow with more ease.

CHAPTER 6 – "CRAZY MIKE DID IT!"

Remember, the real purpose of any admissions essay is to help the reader get to know you—your passions, your humor, your grace and determination—as well some little "quirks" that make you who you are. In Chapter 5, I called this your genius, but, while showing your genius, you don't need to sound like a smartypants. You just need to sound like you.

We all have distinct and recognizable ways of talking; in writing we can create that voice on the page. Because I love examples, let's take Tina Fey, the comedian and writer. In her best-selling book, *Bossypants,* she writes about having been slashed by an attacker when she was a kid. Even with this serious subject matter, her humorous voice comes through:

> "But I will tell you this: My scar was a miniature form of celebrity. Kids knew who I was because of it. Lots of people liked to claim they were there when it happened. I was there. I saw it. Crazy Mike did it!
>
> Adults were kind to me because of it. Aunts and family friends gave me Easter candy and oversize Hershey's Kisses long after I was too old for presents. I was made to feel special."

On the other hand, in his autobiography *Open*, tennis pro Andre Agassi's voice feels much more introspective. He stares in the mirror and reflects on his childhood:

> "Whoever I might be, I'm not the boy who started this odyssey, and I'm not even the man who announced three months ago that the odyssey was coming to an end. I'm like a tennis racket on which I've replaced the grip four times and the strings seven times—is it accurate to call it the same racket? Somewhere in those eyes, however, I can still vaguely see the boy who didn't want to play tennis in the first place, the boy who wanted to quit, the boy who did quit many times. I see that golden-haired boy who hated tennis, and I wonder how he would view this bald man, who still hates tennis and yet still plays. "

DO YOU HEAR VOICES?

How did Fey and Agassi create such different voices? Well there's word choice, of course. While Fey uses language the evokes a school playground, "Crazy Mike did it!", Agassi makes choices that reflect how much tennis has permeated his life, comparing himself to racket in which the "grip" and "strings" have been replaced. Perhaps you've got a lexicon all your own. Do you call sandwiches "grinders" or know all the terminology of paleontology? What words come as second nature? The point is to use words that you know and love.

Beyond word choice, there's something else that makes voice come through, and it's sentence structure. Tina Fey's short punchy sentences are funny, while Agassi uses longer more complex sentences, with poetic repetitions and variations. For example, he writes "I'm not the boy [...] I'm not even the man..." to create layers of emotion, spanning anger, bewilderment, and regret.

CAN I HEAR MY VOICE?

READ BEFORE YOU WRITE!

Pick up any memoir or autobiography, or choose one from our recommended list, and you'll "hear" a different voice. Much as a painter might first study the work of a master, see if you can you can learn by exploring word choices and finding patterns in sentence structure. Even a few minutes of reading attentively before writing can yield amazing results.

10-MINUTE TASK FOR THE AMBITIOUS

After reading, spend just a few more minutes imitating another writer's voice. Your content should be completely different as it is the structure of sentences you want to mimic.
Here's a memoirist I love, Mary Karr, in the opening of her memoir *Lit*:

> "Age seventeen, stringy-haired and halter-topped, weighing in the high double digits and unhindered by a high school diploma, I showed up at the Pacific Ocean, ready to seek my fortune with a truck full of extremely stoned surfers. My family, I thought them to be, for such was my quest—a family I could stand alongside pondering the sea. We stood as the blue water surged toward us in six-foot coils."

Wow. Personally, I'd never think to line up words in the way she does, but I'm willing to give it a try. Below is my rendition, which won't make it into an actual essay because it's got Karr's voice not mine. However, the exercise helps me improve as a writer by showing me the choices I habitually make when I order words in a sentence. I'm now inspired to make considered choices, (though I won't consider using "extremely stoned surfers" in a college application essay, no matter how accurate the image is!) and expand the range of my voice.

> "Age fifteen, my hair in a careful bob and beads slung from my neck, unhindered by a real understanding of history, I joined my friends for our first Great Gatsby Party, ready to roar with the twenties. My best friend, who remains my best friend to this day—a friend who would write in my yearbook, 'They're a rotten crowd, you're worth the whole damn bunch put together.' She showed up in boa, and the crowd seemed to part, as she taught us to do the Charleston."

DO I SOUND LIKE ME?

Find your own flow, and read aloud as you revise your drafts. Ask yourself again and again: does this sound like me? And, could I sound better? Now, go forth—read before you write, read aloud what you've written—and find your voice!

CHAPTER 7 – **BE THE HERO OF YOUR OWN STORY**

OK, now that you've had fun with images and voice, it's time to get a little more serious. I often call this moment the big "SO WHAT?" So what if you forded Snake River, carved a winning pumpkin, or interned at a Congressional office? Why should the reader care?

The answer is simple: because it's meaningful to you. And what makes a story, or a life, meaningful? Undoubtedly, it's a journey. You begin in one place and end somewhere different, no longer the same person that you were at the start.

To find the SO WHAT of your story, you must, at some level, find yourself as a hero. As Irena mentioned in her introduction, many traditional heroes descend into a dark underworld; others—think Holden Caulfield, Scout Finch, or Cora (in Colson Whitehead's *Underground Railroad*)—journey to prep schools, courthouses, forests, or the depths of their own ideas. They put their ingenuity, courage, and resolve to the test, and emerge, perhaps triumphant, perhaps not, but certainly not the same person who started out. This may sound daunting, but simply put, you should be able to answer the question: *how did I change?*

Change, after all, is what makes a good story. Think about all that reading you've done in English class and for fun. Whether the protagonist is Harry Potter or Jane Eyre, they certainly developed and grew. Now is your chance to be a hero, too.

Before you set to scribbling about your struggles with villains, traumatic accidents, or alien forces threatening life as we know it, keep in mind that heroism comes in all shapes and sizes. Quiet discoveries and small shifts in thinking are often more meaningful than big adventures or obvious achievements. The rest of your application may be full of the "what" of accomplishments, but it is who you were before and who you became as a result of your experiences that engages your essay readers.

WHAT LED YOU TO BE WHO YOU ARE TODAY?

It may help to go back to Chapter 4 to get you thinking. In that exercise, others reflected back your own best qualities— generosity? wit? grit? leadership? But were you always this way?

At this point you may already have a story in mind. Perhaps you're writing about leading your crew team, or training a guide dog, or babysitting your nephew. Whatever it is, ask yourself what you were like before this experience and how you changed as a result.

DISCOVER YOUR JOURNEY, EASY AS 1-2-3

Step One – "I used to _____, but now I _____. "
Fill in the blanks at least three times, for example:

1. I used to eat mac 'n cheese for lunch every day, but now I teach cooking classes at a summer camp.
2. I used to play violin in my school's orchestra, but now I am more interested in science.
3. I used to stay silent in Spanish class, but now I'm more outgoing in Spanish than in English.

Step Two – Transform each simple statement into the overview of a journey.

1. A journey from eating only mac 'n cheese to studying and teaching nutrition to wanting to pursue a medical degree.
2. A journey from recognizing the interwoven parts of a beautiful symphony to exploring the fundamental matter of the universe through the lens of physics.
3. A journey from being an outgoing child, who used language and humor to gain attention and connect with others, to a shy middle schooler in a new bilingual school who learned to embrace new and joyful ways to communicate.

Step Three – Expand the overview into an insightful essay.
Each overview you created is a secret map, and the essay itself is a journey. Take the reader's hand and pull her along by using suspense and letting events unfold without much explanation. Small insights can arrive like breadcrumbs on a trail, but your bigger insights should be saved for the end. Don't be surprised if

your essay evolves as you write it and no longer matches your overview. Maybe you used to think you knew the real topic of your college essay, but along the way you've discovered something better!

EXTRA TIP: HIGHLIGHT THE LOWLIGHTS

Remember almost every journey, in literature as in life, has a nadir, or a low point—don't be afraid to present a moment of real loneliness, frustration or disconnection at some point in your journey. Then be sure to move on. Challenge yourself to discover how your struggles have brought with them valuable lessons.

NOW, GET THIS JOURNEY STARTED

You've used the 1-2-3 process to generate simple statements, develop engaging overviews, and to ponder the how each overview might become an essay map. Now, pull out your compass and get started! Admissions readers are excited to follow your journey.

CHAPTER 8 – **REFINING YOUR MAP**

Great! You've brainstormed ideas, you've discovered a topic, you've found your voice, you've conveyed a personal journey, but somehow your essay doesn't feel done. And, most likely, it isn't. Now comes the art of revision.

BEWARE OF MISLEADING ADVICE

At this stage in the process you'll likely share your essay with someone else. As all writers know, this is a risky venture. You might get great feedback, but you may also hear a version of one of these four dark horsemen:

1. "This is great!"
2. "You just need a comma here. (Otherwise, this is great!)"
3. "Are you sure you want to write about your favorite cowboy boots?" or "...Half Price Books?" or "... your artisan pickles?"
4. "What about your leadership in student council, can't you just sneak that in somehow?"

My responses, just for the record:

1. It is always nice to be supported, but general praise for a writer is not very useful. Ask your reader what details, phrases or ideas they specifically enjoyed. This may help you to know what to keep when you revise.
2. Correct punctuation and spelling are of course critical when you are submitting your essay, but focusing on minutiae too soon will distract you from your primary mission: an

authentic and engaging essay. So, thank your eagle-eyed reader, and then ask her if she can also paraphrase the "story" of the essay. This will help you determine if your writing is conveying all that you hope to convey.

3. Smile and answer, "Yes!" If a topic is meaningful and interesting to you, you will almost certainly do a better job creating meaning and interest for the reader.

4. Well-meaning, but perhaps the worst of all, is feedback that encourages you to slip in generically common achievements to market yourself. Assure your nervous reader (or parent) you've got that covered, and you'll include the missing strength elsewhere in your application.

So what should you do once you have a first draft? Here's a simple idea that I've found helpful again and again:

BE AGILE AND UPDATE YOUR OUTLINE

An outline is a map you lay out before you write. Some of you may have started your essay by drafting such a map, some of you may have simply written your way in. Either way, let's now think about outlines as a guide for revision.

As you know, the process of writing is really rewriting. That's why it is important to look back to find the right and wrong turns, the high points and the bumps, and then refine your map. If you have a first draft, no matter how rough, try this out.

Step One - Slowly and aloud

Read through your essay. Slowly. And, aloud. (And in your voice). You'll be surprised at what you notice!

Step Two - A simple outline

Sketch a simple summary-style outline of the essay progression—no need for Roman numerals or even complete sentences. Here is a actual student example:

> **Intro:** Anecdote about me playing the Mad Hatter in the school play.
>
> **Body Para 1:** I'd only worked backstage before, this was my first attempt for a role. When I won it, I was surprised. Thanks to my theater friends I had the courage to audition.
>
> **Body Para 2:** Flashback to who I was when I started HS, a nervous newcomer at my city's largest public school and someone who had never even been to the theater. I kind of thought actors were full of themselves. Now I know it takes a lot more than ego to get up on stage.
>
> **Conclusion:** Trying out and happily winning the goofiest role. Watching my friends cheer me on, going to my first cast party.

Step Three - Consider the beauty of chronology

When we first draft an essay, more and more ideas may pour out as we write. It's important that we get them all down in what the writer Anne Lamott calls a "sh*#ty first draft." Details come to us as we write, and, in our minds, we no doubt make perfect sense. But on closer inspection, the order of events may be unnecessarily jumbled. Find the trouble spots—where jumping back and forth in time confuses rather than clarifies or builds suspense—and temporarily pull out sentences that disrupt the essay's flow.

Step Four - A new map

Make a new outline that adheres more closely to chronological order. This doesn't mean that you can't flashback or use other fun techniques, but it does mean that you have to be aware, each step of the way, about what happened first, and second, and third.

Intro: Anecdote about me playing the Mad Hatter in the school play

Body Para 1: Flashback to who I was when I started HS, a nervous newcomer at my city's largest public school and someone who had never even been to the theater. (I might joke that it "wasn't my cup of tea.")

Body Para 2: Meeting friends who were self-proclaimed "drama-ramas" my sophomore year; attending plays, joining the tech crew, making costumes and working backstage. Details that show growing friendships and self-confidence along the way.

Conclusion: Trying out for the fall play junior year and happily winning an oddball role. Realizing there was more to theater than I thought; that it involved collaboration, authenticity and selflessness. That it took a lot more than "ego" to get up on stage. I grew to understand that performing under pressure is something I am surprisingly good at.

NOW PUT YOUR REVISED MAP TO USE

Use your newly improved map as a revision guide. Cut and paste, rewrite, revise, and add details and insights. Putting one foot in front of the other, you're bound to end up with a clearer, more engaging, and authentic draft two. Repeat the process again and again, and you will find your way to a successful college application essay!

CHAPTER 9 – **PLOTTING (not plodding!) ALONG**

In Chapter 8, I suggested that straight-forward chronological narrative is a great friend to personal essay writers. Now, let's take the revision idea one step further. Certainly we can all easily relay events in chronological order. Here's what I did this morning:

> "I got up at dawn. I took a walk. I met a neighbor. She'd lost her cat."

My list may tell a story, but it's not an engaging one. The events need to be connected—to each other and to an overall purpose—in order to create meaning.

MAKING CONNECTIONS

You might think of connections as causality, or, in fiction-writing terms, plot. In *Aspects of the Novel*, the writer E.M. Forster makes a clear distinction between a basic story and a story with plot. I love his simple example:

> **Story:** "The king died, and then the queen died."
> **Story with plot:** "The king died, and then the queen died of grief."

Which version is more compelling? The second!

Plot is what tugs us along, creates connections, and makes us want to read more. We don't just simply have facts any more, we now have reasons.

So how does this apply to your essay? Your essay should have purpose, and purpose is revealed through meaningful connections.

CONNECTING TO YOUR PURPOSE

Now challenge yourself to sum up the the main purpose of your essay. For example,

1. To show how learning photography helped me observe the world more carefully.
2. To reveal how my leadership of a current events club encouraged me to grow more confident and aware of the world.
3. To express how my chocolate-making hobby opened my mind to the wonders of chemistry.

Once you are pretty clear about your purpose (you don't have to be 100% clear!), comb through your draft and look for sentences that don't quite connect. For example, the photography and observation essay might have a sentence that reads something like:

> "I took lots of pictures of my younger brother. He hated them all. "

We might chuckle at this line, and it is certainly believable. But is it relevant to a well-plotted narrative? A clearer connection to the essay's purpose is just waiting to be made.

> "I took lots of pictures of my younger brother. When they were developed, I saw new aspects of his character: the mischief in his eyes, the frustrated furrow of his brow, and the joy in his toothless grin."

Note: The brother's reaction could still come into play, but it may not be needed at all.

CONNECTING EVENTS WITH "WHY"

Remember the queen in Forster's example? She didn't simply die for no reason; she died because she was grieving for the king.

In an essay draft, it is easy to find weak connections where causality can be clarified. Here's another example of a narrative in need of more plot.

> "The first day in my tenth grade world geography class, I couldn't find Syria on the map. I formed a current events club."

In the writer's mind, the connection is probably clear, but why not let the reader in on it? A simple way to remedy the problem is to ask and answer the question "why?"

> "In my tenth grade world geography class, I was mortified to discover that I couldn't find Syria on the map, and neither could half of my peers. Responsibility and curiosity stirred inside me, and I started reading news blogs each morning. Once I'd learned more, I realized how much more there was to know and share, so I formed a current events club."

Grammar Tip: Introductory clauses help to show causality. In both of the above revisions, notice the introductory clauses:

> "When they were developed, I saw...."
> "Once I'd learned more, I realized..."

Causality is built right into this structure. Go ahead, try it!

> When _____, I saw _____
> Once _____, I realized _____

CONNECTING YOUR READER AND YOU

If you push yourself to repeatedly ask and answer the question "why?" you'll better understand the meaning of your story, and, the more you understand, the more you can refine your draft to help the reader get it, too. That, in a nutshell, is just what you're aiming for: in your college application essay, as in life, it's great to be understood!

CHAPTER 10 – **IRENA'S GUIDE TO LOVING WORDS — AND LETTING THEM GO**

When Laurie and I work with students, I am often the scalpel-wielding last stop before an essay is completed, which is rather ironic considering that as a high school senior, I was selected "Most Likely to Talk to Anyone or Anything about Anyone or Anything." I love words. I love words more than anything. To this day, I love to tell long, complicated stories with tangents (in fact, my tangents often have tangents, and those tangents will occasionally sprout mini-digressions, like a verbal Hydra). But then, somewhere along the way, I discovered the power of brevity.

BREVITY IS THE SOUL OF WIT

Granted, it was one of the most prolix characters in literature who said that, but still: the power of the short, punchy sentence, of the point made elegantly and well, of surgically precise narrative concision is undeniable. You've experienced this power if you've ever been exposed to the meticulously crafted advertising tagline— "Just Do It," for instance—or if you ever came across a line of poetry so finely honed it made you squint in surprise and pleasure ("Because I could not stop for death / He kindly stopped for me"). One of the most powerful sentences in the English language only has two words: "Jesus wept." Go slightly higher on the verbosity scale, and it's amazing how much people can pack into six words in the Six Word Memoir Project.

Have you ever tried to sum up anything in six words? I dare you to try. It's mind-bendingly difficult and surprisingly fun.

When I began working with high school seniors completing college applications, I didn't so much discover brevity as have brevity foisted on me, by way of essay word count restrictions. How do you help someone condense their rich, complicated, textured essence of who they are into 650 words? Or 250 words? Or 100?

> **MIT:** Tell us something you do for the pleasure of it, 100 words. Go. OK, now stop.

CUT WHAT PEOPLE SKIP

Here's what I tell my students: first write a lot, and then cut everything that's not important. Cut ruthlessly. Cut to the bone. (Or, to paraphrase Elmore Leonard, try to leave out the parts that people tend to skip.) You can't know what's important until you've written a lot (one of the many reasons the first draft is also known as the "vomit first draft"), and you'll know what's important when a sentence or a word clutches at your shirt and refuses to be dismissed.

BE BRUTAL

For everything else, cut. An old school editor once described this process as "murdering your darlings," and yes, it feels exactly as brutal as that. But sometimes, you have to make sacrifices. Yes, a sentence may be pretty, and yes, you may have honed and polished and revised and sweated over each word, but if it's not moving your story forward, it's gotta go.

TRUST YOUR READER

If you have three or four instances that demonstrate your humor, your energy, your tenacity, your curiosity, pick the best one and axe the others. The last example standing won't capture you in your entirety, but it will give your readers a sense of who you are, just as a synecdoche deploys a single, limited designation to stand for a larger whole ("The White House" for the presidency, "hands" for helpers, "boots on the ground" for army, to name just a few). Take it on faith that the example you chose—you must have chosen it for a reason—will resonate more powerfully than you think. Trust that your reader will read between the lines.

Here's what else you can cut without a second thought:

- Sentences full of abstractions that anyone else could have written. You know the ones. Soccer can teach anyone persistence, discipline, and resilience. Only you know what it feels like to take a ball to the face.

- The long lead-up: "First I became interested in bioengineering, then I emailed some professors, some of whom never bothered to email me back. Others responded but said they were too busy. Finally, months later, I entered the lab of Professor X." Instead, try this: "When I first walked into Professor X's laboratory..."

- The phrases "To begin," "Subsequently," and "In conclusion." You're telling a story, not debating an opponent in Lincoln-Douglas. Let the story unfold.

- Most adverbs. Adverbs are a crutch. Strong verbs can stand on their own two feet, thank you very much, and they contain multitudes. Which is better: ran quickly or sprinted? Laughed uproariously or guffawed? Hit hard (or, even worse, hit really hard) or pounded? Looked carefully or scrutinized?

- The words "very," "really," or "interesting."

- Passive voice or subservient mention of your own incredible luck at meeting this or that luminary, as in "I was lucky to be able to meet...." How about, "I met"? With all the freed-up space, you can tell us what you actually talked about!

- Over-explaining. Consider these two sentences:
  "I took a deep breath and kicked the ball. It arced across the field, a streaking comet, hit the crossbar, and bounced harmlessly away."
  Or
  "I took a deep breath and kicked the ball. It arced across the field, a streaking comet, hit the crossbar, and bounced harmlessly away. I was devastated."

Do you really need the third sentence? I would argue—strenuously (yes, I know what I said about adverbs, but this is an exception that proves the rule)—that you do not. Leaving things unsaid opens up an imaginative space where your essay can breathe, where your readers can connect with you, where they can feel their own punch-to-the-gut disappointment without you taking them, step by step, through the five stages of missing-the-goal grief. Give your readers credit; they'll figure it out. If you're really tight on space, you can probably cut the "streaking comet," too.

USE A SCALPEL

Taking a scalpel to your own writing can feel as harrowing as taking a scalpel to your own skin. These words came out of you; you pored over them, maybe (even with the aid of a thesaurus); you read them to yourself, hunched over your keyboard—and now some of them will have to go.

If the prospect brings you unbearable pain (and if you've invested the kind of emotional and intellectual energy in your essays that you should have, it will), save the longer version in a different draft. Title it "For my memoir." And then think about what's truly important—what only you know, what only you can say—and cut everything else. The delete key can be your most powerful tool, but that doesn't mean you can't still love words. It just means you need to let some of them go.

Trust me. And just do it.

CHAPTER 11 – *DON'T PANIC!*

We've talked about your genius and about self-reflection, we've talked about voice and images and plot. You've gotten tips on revision and editing. But maybe you've skimmed through and nothing has quite clicked. Or your hard drive died. Or you wrote about your trip to Central America, and so did everyone else. Or you finally finished your Common App essay, and now you have SO MANY supplements. You're starting over. It happens.

In the immortal words of Douglas Adams, *don't panic*! If you feel pressed for time, these easy 10-minute steps will get you going.

THE FIVE-STEP PLAN

The good news? You can start where you're at, which is already on your way. After all, you've been living for seventeen or more years, you've got plenty of stories to tell.

Step 1 - Get centered

Take a walk, listen to music, or just close your eyes for a few minutes. Recall experiences in your life that relate to the prompt you're writing about. And, yes, even if the prompt is about a global issue or asks the enigmatic "Why Our School?" question, begin with yourself. When did you face a challenge, or learn something new? What big influences have shaped your life? Let yourself drift into memories. Where are you? Who are you with? What are you doing? Write for 10 minutes.

Step 2 - Let it unfold

Read what you wrote (and read it aloud). Is there a story emerging? Let things unfold in a "first-this-and-then-that" chronological order. Continue to integrate details that help the reader to stand in your shoes. Write for 10 more minutes.

Step 3 - Outline what you have

Again, read what you wrote. Now sketch an outline of your essay in progress. Does your essay have a purpose or a theme? Write one sentence that sums up what you think your essay is about. Compare that statement to the prompt. Do they connect? Adjust your purpose as needed. Now, to reflect your refined purpose, create a new outline. OK, so this may take a little longer than 10 minutes, but no need to overthink it!

Step 4 - Start over, but not from scratch

Open a new document. Without copying and pasting, write your essay again. As you write, you may find that those parts of your draft that connect best with your theme stick, while others drift away. Add more details that reflect the new outline you've created. Write for at least 10 minutes.

Step 5 - Wrap it up

Read your draft again and ask yourself SO WHAT? Your answer is your essay's conclusion. Draft that conclusion—you guessed it, in 10 minutes!—and graft it to the end of your essay. Et voilà, you have a solid college application essay well underway.

CHAPTER 12 – **WHY *US*?**

You've composed drafts, refined outlines, and revised to produce vivid and engaging self-portraits. But now you're faced with a tough supplementary essay, one that seems to ask less about who you are, and more about the uncertain future: the prompt in which your school of choice asks, Why *Us*?

DIG DEEP

You may find that you're scratching your head. Maybe the only thing that comes to mind is that you really want to live in New York, or Chicago, or Austin. Maybe you know this school has a really good reputation, but you're not sure for what exactly. You go to the "about" page of their website and find yourself channeling their message and writing:

> "George Mason is Virginia's largest public research university, and its setting the benchmark for a bold, progressive education that serves the needs of students and communities."

Uh oh. You know this isn't what you want to say, but what do you want to say? Here's a way to help uncover it.

THE 50/50 RULE

As an admissions specialist, Irena tipped me off to this rule years ago. It's pretty simple. As you write your essay about why you want to attend a particular school, think about proportion: 50% about you / 50% about them. (And, here's the secret: even the half about them is really about you, specifically how you envision yourself as a student on their campus.) Then find a theme that connects the two halves into one glorious on-point whole.

LET'S GET STARTED

Step 1 - Look into their sites
Take 30 minutes and poke around the school's website, Facebook page, etc. If you were lucky enough to tour the campus, jot down

what you remember most from your visit. Dig deep into areas that interest you: courses, clubs, lecture series, service groups, research opportunities, study abroad, and more. Have fun imagining your future life. Bookmark a few pages and take a few notes.

Now, write a sentence: "I can't wait to xxx, yyy, and zzz as a student at..." It's OK to write a few different versions and to dream big. Don't cut yourself off by thinking, "but I could never...".

On the other hand, be authentic—you probably won't be playing college golf if you've never picked up a club.

Step 2 - Research their mission
A mission statement expresses a school's core values, and these values have often been labored over in long committee meetings. So find it, read it, and write a sentence about the aspect of the school's stated mission that you most admire. This is a simple way to find what beliefs you share with the school.

For example, imagine you look at Cornell's mission and find the idea of "thinking otherwise." Do you like what they say about creative collaboration and bottom up thinking?

Now, see if your examples from Step 1 can connect with your understanding of their mission. For example, if you're focusing on a collaborative environment, you might write, "I can't wait to team up with other students in the Space Initiative and collaborate and compete in NASA-sponsored events."

Step 3 - Dig into your life

Given your responses in Step 1 and Step 2, look to your own experience to see how who you are already connects with how you imagine your life at the school of your choice. If you're interested in their community impact program, have you already volunteered in your own community? If you want to study abroad in Oaxaca, Mexico, have you already taken Spanish or expressed an interest in street art like Oaxacan murals? If you love their core curriculum, have you already discovered the pleasures of the Socratic method? If you value the school's spirit of collaboration and quirky innovation, did you form an alt-funk band or an improv group with friends?

The connections are endless and, remember, they don't have to be taken straight from your resume. College admission is as much about your intellectual experience as it is about your community service. Feel free to reference classes you've taken, research you've done, your fascination with NOVA and the like.

Step 4 - ACK, a thesis statement

Write a personal thesis statement. I know, I know, a THESIS? Don't worry. You don't even need to include the statement in your essay, but it can help guide you. Your thesis should show how you and the school are a perfect match. Extending on our previous example, "I've always learned the most when given a problem and a smart team of friends to help me solve it, and, at XYZ University, I know I'll be encouraged to collaborate and discover..." would hit the mark with a school which prioritizes teamwork.

Step 5 - One paragraph at a time

OK, you have gathered your notes, statements, and ideas. Now it's time to bring it all together. Draft a paragraph about you, your beliefs, and your intellectual and community engagement. End with a statement about who you are in the world and who you hope to become at your school of choice. Draft a second paragraph which demonstrates the intersection of your interests and the school's opportunities and write yourself into their culture.

THREE WARNING SIGNS

1. Location? Location? Location?

Notice I did not say suggest that you mention how excited you would be to live in a particular city. Unless you're talking about university/city partnerships in the form of internships or volunteer programs, I'd skip it. Ditto to generic references to their beautiful campus. This note from Chapman University basically sums up how most admissions readers feel:

> "We're looking for specifics here! What separates Chapman from the other institutions you're considering? What special programs, activities and aspects of campus are most attractive and compelling to you? We're well aware that our campus is in an interesting location and is aesthetically

pleasing—dig a little deeper to show us you know why Chapman could be a great fit for you!"

2. Marketing language?

Do the adjective test! Do you sound like a brochure? Smith College doesn't need to hear that they are "Individual. Global. Exceptional." That marketing language is aimed at *you*. Tell them something they don't know, something specific about your connection to their school.

3. Fishing for authenticity?

After all of this effort, are you still coming up dry? Ask yourself the tough question: Do I REALLY want to apply here? The application process is full of twists and turns, and there are many great choices. If you aren't finding it easy to show the love, consider letting go, thus freeing your mind and resources for a better chance elsewhere!

CHAPTER 13 – **KEEP YOUR EYE ON THE PRIZE**

As you may have noticed, we live in a time of great distraction: school commitments, friendship drama, social media, politics, you name it. Truth be told, there is plenty to keep you away from the task of writing your essays. So, how do you stay focused during the final laborious stretch? You could go back and read Chapter 1 again, but, let me help distill it for you.

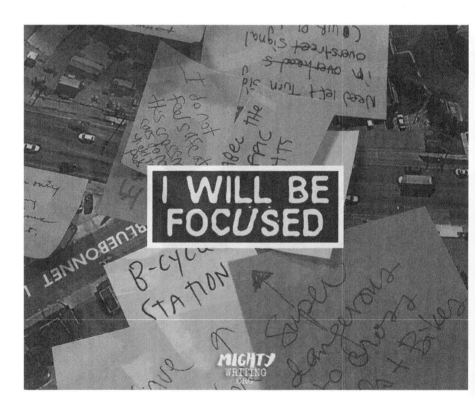

Separate

To keep your eye on the prize, you may need to be selfish. It is a good time to say NOPE. Turn off your phone, turn on some non-distracting music. Or find a quiet place like a library where you can work alone, where you parents aren't hovering and your friends aren't texting, and where the news of the world, for a solid hour, won't reach you. Your future deserves this much, so claim some space for you.

Buddy Up

Claim time for you, but don't go it alone. Pick a reliable friend who is also applying to college, push each other along, and set deadlines to share your drafts. This will help you stay on task and on time.

Set Deadlines

Know your due date(s) and allow for four or five revisions. Seriously. For example, if you need to submit by Dec. 21, and it takes you an average of four days to revise, your first deadline should be Dec. 5. So get writing! When asking for feedback, use the tips in Chapter 8 to help you along.

Pace Yourself

If you can't find enough time and space, then try setting a pace. Start with 10-15 minutes a day. Wake up a little earlier, commit yourself to using your off periods at at school, or use writing as an excuse to get out of after dinner clean up!

Warm Up

Just as athletes gear up and get psyched in preparation for a game, writers need to shift their brains into the right mode. It's not adrenaline you're after but something more like dopamine, a pleasant urge to take action and move forward. And there's nothing like the rush of a good read. Reread something you wrote and are proud of, enjoy a chapter from a favorite novel, or dip into our recommended reading at http://mightywriting.org/resources.

Repurpose

Don't let previous work go to waste! Maybe you wrote a response to the University of Texas prompt: "Most students have an identity, an interest, or a talent that defines them in an essential way..." Now University of California has given you eight prompts from which to choose. Look carefully at your choices. "What would you say is your greatest talent or skill?" is basically the same question that you answered for UT. But the word limit is different? No problem. Simply reread Irena's Chapter 10 on concision and trim your material down to size.

Remember

Your schedule might feel packed but there's a light at the end of the tunnel. Committing yourself now means enjoying yourself later. And there's nothing more enjoyable than college acceptance! So take a deep breath, say NO to some other commitment, and simply get going.

After all, it's your life, full of heartfelt, surprising, insightful, and mighty stories just waiting to be shared by you, a Mighty Writer.

ABOUT THE AUTHORS

Laurie Filipelli

Laurie's journey as a writer started in second grade when her poem "Snow in Spring" was featured on the school bulletin board. She is now the author of two collections of poems, Elseplace (Brooklyn Arts Press, 2013) and Girl Paper Stone (forthcoming in 2018 from Black Lawrence Press), as well as numerous personal essays. Laurie holds an M.F.A from Indiana University and an M.A. from the University of Cincinnati. In her two decades as an educator, she has taught college writing classes, high school English, and served as education programs manager and curriculum developer for Badgerdog Literary Publishing, a writers-in-the-schools nonprofit.

As an independent writing coach and in collaboration with Irena Smith, Laurie specializes in providing college application essay writing guidance, helping countless students find their way toward admission into top-tier schools while discovering the self-knowledge needed to succeed in college and beyond. **Discover more writing tips and learn about her services at MightyWriting.org. Stay in touch at Facebook.com/MightyWriting.**

Irena Smith

Irena holds a Ph.D. in Comparative Literature from UCLA and has taught humanities and composition at UCLA, Stanford, and Notre Dame de Namur University. From 1999 to 2003, she read applications at Stanford's Office of Undergraduate Admission, and for the past 10 years, has been working as an independent admissions consultant in the San Francisco Bay Area. Her work focuses on helping students understand how all the components of their application—the transcript, teacher letters of recommendation, activity lists, and, of course, the essays—tell a story, and identify ways in which students can bring all the elements together to craft their most compelling narrative.

She blames her obsession with stories in all forms on her parents, who, in spite of encouraging her to pursue an engineering degree, instilled a love of reading from an early age and taught her that a house can never have too many books.

Made in the USA
Las Vegas, NV
19 July 2024